Investment Banking

The Basic Investor's Library

Alternative Investments

Bonds, Preferred Stocks, and the Money Market

Careers in the Investment World

Growth Stocks

Investing and Trading

Investment Banking

Investments and the Law

Mutual Funds

Reading the Financial Pages

Stock Options

The Principles of Technical Analysis

Understanding A Company

Wall Street—How It Works

What Is a Share of Stock?

Chelsea House Publishers

Investment Banking

RACHEL S. EPSTEIN

Paul A. Samuelson
Senior Editorial Consultant

CHELSEA HOUSE PUBLISHERS   New York   Philadelphia

Editor-in-Chief   Nancy Toff
Executive Editor   Remmel T. Nunn
Managing Editor   Karyn Gullen Browne
Copy Chief   Juliann Barbato
Picture Editor   Adrian G. Allen
Art Director   Giannella Garrett
Manufacturing Manager   Gerald Levine

Staff for INVESTMENT BANKING
Senior Editor   Marjorie P. K. Weiser
Associate Editor   Andrea E. Reynolds
Assistant Editor   Karen Schimmel
Editorial Assistant   Tara P. Deal
Copyeditor   James Guiry
Picture Researcher   Ilene Cherna Bellovin
Senior Designer   Laurie Jewell
Designers   Barbara Bachman, Ghila Krajzman
Production Coordinator   Joe Romano

Creative Director   Harold Steinberg

Contributing Editor   Robert W. Wrubel
Consulting Editor   Shawn Patrick Burke

3   5   7   9   8   6   4   2
Library of Congress Cataloging in Publication Data

Epstein, Rachel S.
   Investment banking.

(The Basic investor's library)
   Bibliography: p.
   Includes index.
   Summary: One in a fourteen-volume series, this volume
explains the role of investment banking in the business
world, the concepts of underwriting and issuing stocks
and bonds, and mergers.
   1. Investment banking—Juvenile literature.
[1. Investment banking.   2. Stocks.   3. Bonds]
I. Title.   II. Series.
HG4534.E67   1988   332.66   87-18194
ISBN 1-55546-630-3
      0-7910-0315-9 (pbk.)

CONTENTS

Learning the Tools of Investing

PAUL A. SAMUELSON

W hen asked why the great financial house of Morgan had been so successful, J. Pierpont Morgan replied, "Do you suppose that's because we take money seriously?"

Managing our personal finances is a serious business, and something we all must learn to do. We begin life dependent on someone else's income and capital. But after we become independent, it is a remorseless fact of nature that we must not only support ourselves for the present but must also start saving money for retirement. The best theory of saving that economists have is built upon this model of *life-cycle saving*: You must provide in the long years of prime working life for what modern medicine has lengthened to, potentially, decades of retirement. This life-cycle model won a 1985 Nobel Prize for my MIT colleague Franco Modigliani, and it points up the need to learn the rudiments of personal finance.

Learning to acquire wealth, however, is only part of the story. We must also learn to avoid losing what we have acquired. There is an old saying that "life insurance is *sold*, not bought." The same goes for stocks and bonds. In each case, the broker is guaranteed a profit, whether or not the customer benefits from the transaction. Knowledge is the customer's only true ally in the world of finance. Some gullible victims have lost their lifetime savings to unscrupulous sales promoters. One chap buys the Brooklyn Bridge. Another believes a stranger who asserts that gold will quickly double in price, with no risk of a drop in value. Such "con" (confidence) rackets get written up in the newspapers and on the police blotters every day.

I am concerned, however, about something less dramatic than con artists; something that is not at all illegal, but that costs ordinary citizens a thousand times more than outright embezzlement or fraud. Consider two families, neighbors who could be found in any town. They started alike. Each worked equally hard, and had about the same income. But the Smiths have to make do with half of what the Joneses have in retirement income, for one simple reason: The Joneses followed prudent practice as savers and investors, while the Smiths tried to make a killing and constantly bought and sold stocks at high commissions.

The point is, it does matter to learn how financial markets work, and how you can participate in them to your best advantage. It is important to know the difference between *common* and *preferred* stocks, between *convertible* and *zero-coupon* bonds. It is not difficult to find out what *mutual funds* are, and to understand the difference between the successful Fund A, which charges no commission, or "load," and the equally successful Fund B, which does charge the buyer such a fee.

All investing involves risk. When I was a young assistant professor, I said primly to my great Harvard teacher, Joseph Schumpeter: "We should speculate only with money we can afford to lose." He gently corrected me: "Paul, there is no such money. Besides, a speculator is merely an investor who has lost." Did Schumpeter exaggerate? Of course he did, but in the good cause of establishing the basic point of financial management: Good past performance is no guarantee of the future.

That is why *diversification* is the golden rule. "Don't put all your eggs in one basket. And watch all those baskets!" However, diversification does not mean throwing random darts at the financial pages of the newspaper to choose the best stocks in which to invest. The most diversified strategy of all would be to invest in a portfolio containing all the stocks in the comprehensive Standard & Poor's 500 Stock Index. But rather than throw random darts at the financial pages to pick out a few stocks, why not throw a large bath towel at the newspaper instead? Buy a bit of everything in proportion to its value in the larger world: Buy more General Motors than Ford, because GM is the bigger company; buy General Electric as well as GM because the auto industry is just one of many industries. That is called being an *index investor*. Index investing makes sense because 70 out of 100 investors who try to do better than the Standard & Poor's 500, the sober record shows, do worse over a 30-year period.

Do not take my word for this. The second lesson in finance is to be skeptical of what writers and other experts say, and that includes being skeptical of professors of economics. So I wish readers *Bon voyage!* on their cruise to command the fundamentals of investing. On your mainship flag, replace the motto "Nothing ventured, nothing gained" with the Latin words *Caveat emptor*—Let the buyer beware.

Investment Banking

On December 12, 1980, Apple Computer, which five years earlier had helped start the revolution in personal computers, went public. That is, it sold ownership shares of its company—common stock—to investors for the first time.

Steven P. Jobs, age 20, and Stephen G. Wozniak, 24, Apple's founders, had designed the company's first computer in Jobs's bedroom and built it in his family's garage in 1975. By 1980, with sales well over $100 million, Apple was one of the fastest growing small companies in the United States. That year Apple decided to go public. To keep growing, the company would need the large infusion of money that comes from a public offering of stock. Apple's managers believed that because technology stocks were selling at high prices, the company could probably get a good price for its stock.

The public offering brought in $96.8 million and was hailed by more than one expert as one of the hottest offerings of the year. Demand for Apple's shares was so great that the stock price jumped from $22 to $29 on the first day of trading.

Going public is a complex process. Apple had to call on legal and financial specialists to work out the details of issuing stock to the public. Those specialists are known as investment bankers.

THE WORLD OF INVESTMENT BANKING

The founders of Apple Computer, Steven P. Jobs (left) and Stephen G. Wozniak (right), with company president John Sculley, introduce their new portable computer, the Apple IIc, to the public in April 1984.

When stock is sold to the public, an investment banking firm handles many aspects of the transaction. The firm, or usually a group of firms, *underwrites* the stock issue by buying all shares of a company's stock being issued. Then the firm immediately tries to sell the stock to the investing public. Because Apple Computer had arranged with an investment banking firm to underwrite its stock issue, the company knew it would receive a predictable sum of money as a result of going public. Taking on the financial risk of selling new stocks to the public and helping growing companies raise capital is one of the major functions of investment banking firms.

Investment banking firms underwrite *initial public offerings* (IPOs), the first-time sale of a company's stock to the general public. They also underwrite subsequent offerings of stock for companies that are already publicly owned and bond issues for both corporations and state and local governments. To both new and old companies, investment banking firms offer financial advice on such matters as the timing, size, and type of a securities offering; whether a security should be sold only in the United States or also abroad; and how to make a stock attractive to potential investors. Investment banking firms also help companies accomplish or avoid mergers and acquisitions. For such specialized advice and services, investment banking firms charge large fees, and individual investment bankers make a great deal of money.

THE HISTORY OF INVESTMENT BANKING

According to Paul Hoffman in *The Dealmakers*, investment banking is an American invention. The big banking houses of Europe—those of the Rothschilds, Barings, and Hambros—have traditionally used their own money to finance new businesses. In the United States, however, investment banking firms developed as intermediaries that brought together the money of large financial institutions and the needs of growing industries.

In the last half of the 19th century, the two basic elements of investment banking developed: underwriting and syndication.

The building of railroads, steel mills, and water distribution systems that occurred during this period required large amounts of money. The companies doing this building could have tried to raise money by selling millions of shares of stock. Previously, companies had gotten money for expansion by selling their shares themselves. But now so many companies were growing so rapidly, all at the same time, that there was a real danger of flooding the market with more shares than investors wanted to or could buy. This would have lowered the price per share, and the com-

A broker follows stocks on a ticker tape in his office in 1904.

panies would have been unable to raise enough money. Some wealthy people saw an opportunity to gain greater profit in the long run by helping developing industries sell their stock issues in an orderly way. They would underwrite stock issues, guaranteeing a set price per share to the issuing company. They would hold the stock for varying periods of time and assume the risk of reselling it in the market. By controlling the timing of the sale of stock, they hoped to keep investor interest high. A classic example of early underwriting was J. P. Morgan's purchase of 250,000 shares of New York Central Railroad for $120 each from the company owner, William Vanderbilt. Morgan soon sold the shares to a group of London banks for $130 each. Underwriting was obviously profitable for both the companies and the bankers.

Syndication evolved when it became too costly for a single firm to underwrite a large stock issue. Several firms cooperated to underwrite an issue, thus dividing the cost and sharing the financial risk. A *syndicate* consists of several investment banking firms that join together to share the risk of underwriting and reselling shares of a particular issue of stock. In the 19th century syndication helped to distribute shares to the public because some members of syndicates had large networks of salesmen who were in touch with investors throughout the country. Today, too, syndication makes it possible to reach a larger pool of potential investors, the customers of the firms involved.

During World War I, investment bankers helped raise money from the American public to finance the Allies' war effort in Europe. After the war, as the automobile, aviation, radio, and public utility industries began to develop, investment bankers underwrote stock offerings for many new and growing companies. They were joined by commercial bankers who used their depositors' savings to underwrite stock issues that were risky. After almost a decade of frenzied stock speculation, the crash of 1929 occurred when investors pulled their money out of the stock market in a matter of days. Soon hundreds of banks were forced to close, which meant that businesses could not borrow money to meet their operating expenses. Eventually many factories and other businesses closed as well, throwing millions of people out of work.

Government investigations in the early 1930s revealed that many investment and commercial bankers had engaged in illegal and unethical practices, which had contributed to the crash of 1929 and the Great Depression that followed. As a result of the investigations, two changes, designed to prevent such abuses, came to the investment world and continue to influence it today. One was the Glass-Steagall Act, named for its legislative sponsors, which prohibits commercial banks from underwriting the securities of corporations, thus separating investment banking from commercial banking.

The second change was the creation of the Securities and Exchange Commission (SEC), a government agency set up in 1934 to regulate the sale of stocks to the public.

The SEC sees to it that firms that issue and underwrite securities comply with the full disclosure requirements of the Securities Act of 1933 and the Securities Exchange Act of the following year. Companies must now register with the SEC before selling their stock to the public. As part of the registration process, the issuing company must produce an official report. This report, or *prospectus*, prepared with the advice of investment bankers, lawyers, and accountants, must explain everything significant about the company and describe its finances in detail. When the SEC is satisfied with the prospectus, it permits the company to go ahead with its offering.

After a quiet period, investment bankers became active again in the 1950s, as retailers and real estate, aviation, and electronics companies sold new shares to the public. In 1955 General Motors issued $325 million worth of stock. It was the country's largest offering until the next year when the Ford Motor Company, which had been family owned, went public with an offering that was twice as big. In the 1960s investment bankers made money by advising companies on the acquisition of other companies, which resulted in the formation of conglomerates. A *conglomerate* is a large corporation with numerous divisions that produce a variety of products and services.

On May 1, 1975, a new era began on Wall Street. An SEC rule went into effect stating that commissions, the fees paid for business transactions, could no longer be fixed by the New York Stock Exchange (NYSE), as they had been for many years. Instead, commissions were to be negotiated. This meant that customers who traded a huge volume of shares, such as large institutions, could negotiate to reduce the fees they paid to financial firms for their services. The ruling started a new competitiveness on Wall Street and in financial districts around the country.

Investment banking firms expanded to provide additional services to their corporate customers, who were willing to pay well for them. They enlarged their mergers and acquisitions departments, traded stocks for their own accounts, and expanded into international markets. By offering every service a corporate client might want, investment banking firms had a better chance to attract and hold important clients. Before the SEC ruling, clients had stayed with their brokers or investment bankers "for life"; now companies shop around to negotiate the best deal.

In the late 1980s some investment bankers acted unethically and illegally and were indicted for and convicted of activities that are contrary to SEC regulations and various laws. In consequence, some industry experts expect the passage of tough new laws to regulate the financial industry more strictly. But as long as our economy continues to offer opportunities for growth to developing industries, investment bankers will continue to play their important role in the nation's business life.

Brokers trading at the gold commodities market. Investment banking firms have expanded their activities to include serving as commodities brokers.

INVESTMENT BANKING FIRMS

There are a small number of powerful investment banking firms that hold leading positions in the industry. Such firms usually put together the syndicate in a stock issue and underwrite the largest number of shares, thereby receiving the largest commission. These firms also play leadership roles in takeovers, mergers, and acquisitions. The firms in this category are First Boston, Goldman Sachs, Merrill Lynch, Morgan Stanley, Salomon Brothers, and Shearson Lehman Brothers.

A second rank of large investment banking houses, which also play major roles in syndications, includes Bear, Stearns; Dillon, Read; Drexel Burnham Lambert; Kidder, Peabody; Lazard Frères; and Wertheim Schroder. Other firms that offer investment banking services, including

E. F. Hutton, Paine Webber, Prudential-Bache, Smith Barney, Thomson McKinnon, and Dean Witter Reynolds, are better known as retail brokerages.

As a result of deregulation, competition, and mergers, the distinctions between these different types of firms are blurring. A firm that offers investment banking services is also actively trading stocks and bonds both for its own account and for its individual and institutional customers. It may also trade commodities, such as sugar, tin, and cotton. Such a firm will have a research department to determine which industries and companies would be good investments and to learn which companies are likely candidates for merger or acquisition.

Perhaps the outstanding organizational fact about investment banking firms is their flexibility. Good investment banking firms are not bureaucratic. In a successful firm there are many creative people with new ideas. When those ideas require the cooperation of various departments in the firm, several people work together to meet the special needs of clients or investors. This flexibility and creativity bring new revenue to the firm.

There are almost 2,500 broker/dealer firms reporting to the SEC, but only a small number of them are primarily involved in investment banking. It is a small, select world.

UNDERWRITING AND THE CREATION OF SECURITIES

Underwriting, or bringing the stocks and bonds of new and established companies and government agencies to the public, is the primary and traditional function of investment banking firms. Although most firms also offer other services, it is the underwriting of securities that makes investment banking firms unique.

Investment banking firms underwrite initial public stock offerings (IPOs) for corporations, subsequent corporate stock offerings, corporate bonds, and municipal (government agency) bonds. The basic process for underwriting each of these is the same, with slight differences.

An Initial Public Offering

The number of companies going public at any given time reflects the national economy. In 1982, a year of recession (a period of reduced economic activity), there were only 124 IPOs, but the following year there were 686. Two years later, there were 360 IPOs.

A *stock certificate representing 78 shares of stock in Fidelcor, Inc. When a company goes public it offers shares of stock to the public for the first time.*

In an IPO, a privately held corporation—the issuer—sells shares of stock to the public for the first time. This is almost always done through one or more investment bankers who underwrite the shares. The offering is regulated by the SEC. Usually a first-time stock issue is listed on the American Stock Exchange (AMEX) or in the over-the-counter (OTC) market. If the company is large enough, it might meet the requirements for listing on the NYSE. At the time they go public, most companies are corporations whose stock has previously been owned only by a small group of people. This group often includes the founders, relatives of the founders, employees, suppliers, and *venture capitalists* (individuals who provide capital to start or expand a business).

Why Go Public?   When a company goes public, it receives a large and immediate infusion of cash. It may use this money for various corporate purposes, such as buying new factories, equipment, or raw materials; developing new products; or repaying loans borrowed from banks. Sometimes the original owners or investors profit personally as well, if they sell some of their own shares in the public offering.

One reason to go public is that a public company has a better chance than a private one of acquiring more money, either through bank loans, private placements, or bond or stock issues. In addition, public offering of stock makes a company more visible and makes it seem more stable and reliable, which may attract more customers for its products or services.

According to SEC regulations a publicly owned company must file more detailed annual and quarterly reports and issue specific, audited financial statements. Although publishing these reports involves some additional expense for the company, the discipline of regular reporting, which includes following standard accounting practices, is essential for future growth and prosperity.

Three Goldman, Sachs investment bankers outside their New York offices.

The disadvantages of being a public company have to do with the sharing of wealth and control. Suddenly a company that has had only one or a few owners has to answer to all of its investors. Inevitably, some shareholders will be looking only for short-term financial gain and may be indifferent or opposed to plans for long-term development. Going public may also slow down the company's activities because major plans must now receive formal approval from a board of directors. Finally, going public is time consuming and expensive.

The Cast of Characters in an IPO   Several different people and organizations are involved in an IPO. They represent the company, the underwriters, and a variety of outside consultants. The people involved include:

• *Issuing Company's Chief Financial Officer*   The chief financial officer of a company, who is responsible for supervising its financial activities, negotiates with an underwriter about the structure of the underwriting deal. The financial officer knows the needs of the company, and the investment banker knows the needs of the financial markets. The goal is to satisfy both groups as fully as possible.

- *Issuing Company's Outside Counsel* The counsel is a lawyer whose role is to prepare the registration statement, the chief document that must be submitted to the SEC. This lawyer assembles information about the company in the form required and advises the issuing company on how to comply with SEC rules. The lawyer's competence and trustworthiness are crucial to whether the registration statement receives SEC clearance.

- *Independent Certified Public Accountants* The issuer retains an accounting firm that audits the company's financial statements and attests that they correctly present the company's financial position, and that they have been prepared in accordance with generally accepted accounting principles. The financial statements must reflect the results of operations for the past three years.

- *Investment Bankers* Through its corporate finance department, the investment banking firm managing the issue is the company's major financial advisor, working with the company on the structuring of the deal, preparation of documents for the SEC, and pricing the stock to sell in the current market. Through its syndication department, the managing investment banker puts together the group of underwriters who will join in forming the syndicate that will buy the securities from the issuing company and sell them to the public.

- *Investment Banker's Outside Counsel* This lawyer is retained by the investment banker to review the registration statement and other pertinent documents.

- *Securities and Exchange Commission (SEC)* This federal government regulatory body reviews the registration statement and decides whether a company's stock can be sold to the public.

• *State "Blue-Sky" Law Enforcers*   Individual states have enacted "blue-sky" laws to protect investors from being lured into buying issues that have "as much investment potential as a patch of blue sky." Before stock can be sold in a particular state the offering must be checked by state enforcers to see that it complies with the state's blue-sky laws. In some states approval is difficult to obtain, but in others an offering will clear if its registration statement has been satisfactorily reviewed by the SEC.

• *Financial Printer*   The issuer chooses one of the specialized printing firms that have experience with documents designed to meet SEC requirements. Financial printers have the facilities and personnel to print registration statements overnight and deliver them to the SEC in Washington at 9:00 the next morning.

Steps in the Process of Going Public

1. *Preparing the Registration Statement*   The issuer, represented by the company's chief financial officer, the managing underwriter, and all the outside lawyers and accountants work together to produce the *registration statement*. The statement includes a *prospectus*, a formal document describing the company and its financial information, the terms of the offering, whether the original investors will be selling shares, and the intended use of the funds to be raised by the sale of its stock. It contains additional exhibits relevant to the company's operations, such as company employment contracts, leases, bylaws, and the certificate of incorporation. Also in the registration statement is the proposed underwriting agreement between the issuer and the underwriters, which includes such information as the percentage of the company that the issued number of shares will represent and the compensation due to

the underwriters. It usually takes at least a month of very long days to complete the statement. Then it is turned over to the financial printer for printing.

2. *Due Diligence*   This refers to the investigation of the company to determine the accuracy of its prospectus. Everyone involved with the deal must examine the company with due diligence, or particular care. For the underwriters this is especially important. If they perform due diligence according to recognized standards, the firm cannot be held legally liable (for example, in suits by unhappy stockholders) for misstatements or omissions in the prospectus. Due diligence requires that the underwriter visit the company and hold detailed discussions with its managers, accountants, and lawyers. Underwriters also talk to customers and suppliers. Sometimes investment bankers even hire private investigators to help them perform due diligence. Shortly before the registration statement becomes effective, which is usually at least two months from the time it is submitted to the SEC for approval, there is a due diligence meeting at which the underwriters have a final opportunity to question representatives of the company.

3. *Requesting SEC Approval*   When the registration statement is ready, the issuer files it with the SEC. Since the registration statement has not yet been declared "effective," the included prospectus is called a preliminary prospectus or "red herring" (because it has an inscription in red letters on the cover page that indicates the stock cannot be sold until the statement becomes effective). Then the issuer waits, usually about three to six weeks, for SEC comments. The SEC checks the document to make sure that all of the required topics are covered and that standards of "full disclosure" have been met. This means that the registration state-

An analyst visits a company to discuss operations with its chief executive. Representatives of investment banking firms visit companies that are in the process of going public, to verify statements in their prospectuses.

(continued on p. 24)

CASE STUDY OF AN IPO: MICROSOFT GOES PUBLIC

3,095,000 Shares

MICROSOFT.

Microsoft Corporation

Common Stock

Price $21 Per Share

Upon request a copy of the Prospectus describing these securities and the business of the Company may be obtained within any State from any Underwriter who may legally distribute it within such State. The securities are offered only by means of the Prospectus and this announcement is neither an offer to sell nor a solicitation of any offer to buy.

Goldman, Sachs & Co.		Alex. Brown & Sons Incorporated
Bear, Stearns & Co. Inc.	The First Boston Corporation	Dillon, Read & Co. Inc.
Donaldson, Lufkin & Jenrette Securities Corporation	Drexel Burnham Lambert Incorporated	Hambrecht & Quist Incorporated
E. F. Hutton & Company Inc.	Kidder, Peabody & Co. Incorporated	Lazard Frères & Co.
Merrill Lynch Capital Markets	Montgomery Securities	Morgan Stanley & Co. Incorporated
PaineWebber Incorporated	Prudential-Bache Securities	Robertson, Colman & Stephens
L. F. Rothschild, Unterberg, Towbin, Inc.	Salomon Brothers Inc	Shearson Lehman Brothers Inc.
Wertheim & Co., Inc.	Dean Witter Reynolds Inc.	Cable, Howse & Ragen
ABD Securities Corporation	Advest, Inc. Allen & Company Incorporated	Arnhold and S. Bleichroeder, Inc.
Robert W. Baird & Co. Incorporated	Banque de Neuflize, Schlumberger, Mallet	Bateman Eichler, Hill Richards Incorporated
Sanford C. Bernstein & Co., Inc.	William Blair & Company	Blunt Ellis & Loewi Incorporated
Boettcher & Company, Inc.	J. C. Bradford & Co. Butcher & Singer Inc.	Cowen & Co.
Crédit Commercial de France	Dain Bosworth Deutsche Bank Capital Incorporated Corporation	Eberstadt Fleming Inc.
A. G. Edwards & Sons, Inc.	Eppler, Guerin & Turner, Inc.	EuroPartners Securities Corporation
First Southwest Company	Furman Selz Mager Dietz & Birney Incorporated	Gruntal & Co., Incorporated
Hill Samuel & Co. Limited	Howard, Weil, Labouisse, Friedrichs	Interstate Securities Corporation
Janney Montgomery Scott Inc.	Josephthal & Co. Kleinwort, Benson Incorporated Incorporated	Ladenburg, Thalmann & Co. Inc.
Legg Mason Wood Walker Incorporated	McDonald & Company Securities, Inc.	Morgan Grenfell & Co. Limited
Moseley, Hallgarten, Estabrook & Weeden Inc.	The Ohio Company	Oppenheimer & Co., Inc.
Piper, Jaffray & Hopwood Incorporated	Prescott, Ball & Turben, Inc.	Rauscher Pierce Refsnes, Inc.
The Robinson–Humphrey Company, Inc.	Rotan Mosle Inc.	Rothschild Inc.
J. Henry Schroder Wagg & Co. Limited	Sogen Securities Corporation	Stephens Inc.
Stifel, Nicolaus & Company Incorporated	Sutro & Co. Incorporated	Swiss Bank Corporation International Securities Inc.
Thomson McKinnon Securities Inc.		Tucker, Anthony & R. L. Day, Inc.
UBS Securities Inc.	Underwood, Neuhaus & Co. Incorporated	Wheat, First Securities, Inc.

March 14, 1986

Microsoft, a computer software company founded in 1975, was familiar to the computing and investing public by the fall of 1985. Sales in the previous year had totaled $172.5 million, primarily from MS-DOS and PC-DOS, the operating systems that run millions of IBM personal computers and compatible machines.

In 1985 the venture capitalists who had financed Microsoft were not yet pressing for the initial public offering (IPO) that would let them pull out and pocket their gains. Company founder William Gates valued his control of the company more than the money such an offering would bring in.

Microsoft had sold shares of its stock to employees at discount prices and given shares as an inducement to programmers and managers to remain in its work force. The company, although still privately held, had almost 500 shareholders and would soon have to register with the SEC even if it remained private. Because the required registration would be time-consuming and expensive anyway, Microsoft's officers decided that they might as well have a public offering of stock. This would let shareholders who wanted to sell do so. The president liked the idea of going public "when we wanted to, not when we had to."

Microsoft chose Goldman, Sachs as managing underwriter of its IPO, with Alex. Brown as comanaging underwriter.

In mid-December 1985 Microsoft and its attorneys and accountants met with the two managing underwriters and their attorneys. This "all hands" meeting had a 27-point agenda that covered every aspect of the offering, including the amount of money to be raised, the number of shares to be issued, the percentage of outstanding shares that the issue would represent, and the probable opening price of a share. At the time, Gates was aiming for a share price of $15.

In January 1986 Microsoft's outside counsel, with advice and information from the company and the managing underwriters, drafted the prospectus. By the end of the month, the price of the shares was still undecided. Gates suggested a range of $16 to $19 per share, which ultimately went into this prospectus. During this time the comanagers contacted other underwriters to form a syndicate.

On February 1 a messenger rushed the final proof of the preliminary prospectus to the underwriter's lawyer. Two days later Microsoft filed the registration statement with the SEC in Washington, D.C. Meanwhile, the prospective underwriters (eventually 114 firms were part of the syndicate) sent out 38,000 copies of the preliminary prospectus to brokers and institutional investors to solicit interest in the stock while the company waited for the SEC's comments.

To arouse further interest, Goldman, Sachs took Microsoft's top executives on a road show in mid-February. They explained the company and the IPO on the eight-city tour to large audiences of enthusiastic brokers and investors. Because there was so much investor interest and because the stock market was rising, Goldman, Sachs suggested raising the price and issuing more shares than originally planned.

By March 7 the revised prospectus was being proofread at the printer, but price was still an issue. Now Microsoft wanted to raise the stock's price. Goldman, Sachs wanted to open at a price of no higher than $20 to $21. Finally, a compromise price range of $20 to $22 was set. Then the stock market rose sharply, and at a meeting with Goldman, Sachs, the price was set at $21.

The only remaining issue was the *gross spread*, the difference between the stock price to the underwriters and the later price to the public. The spread goes to the underwriters to pay for commissions, expenses, and professional fees. On the afternoon before the day of the offering, Goldman and Microsoft agreed on a spread of $1.31 per share.

The next day, at 8:00 A.M., a courier delivered the complete Microsoft filing package to the SEC. The Microsoft offering was declared effective by the SEC at 9:15 A.M. By 9:35 trading in the stock was "wild." By the end of the day, 2.5 million shares had traded hands, and the price had already risen to $27.75.

A year later Microsoft's shares were trading at more than $90 a share. During May of 1987 Gates sold 520,000 shares of his stock at an average price of $111 per share. He continued to hold almost 40 percent of the company's 26 million outstanding shares. He made almost $58 million in the transactions.

Based on: Bro Uttal, "Inside the Big Deal that Made Bill Gates $350,000,000," *Fortune*, July 21, 1986, pp. 23–33.

(continued from p. 21)

ment contains a complete and clear picture of the company's business and operations. The registration statement is then returned to the company, where it will be revised if necessary to satisfy the SEC's criticisms. When the SEC has no further comments, the issuer sets an offering date and requests the SEC to declare the stock offering effective on that same date.

4. *Requesting State "Blue-Sky" Approval* The issuer submits the revised registration statement in all of the states where the stock will be sold. The goal is to gain state approval by the time the registration statement becomes effective.

5. *Assembling the Syndicate* When the preliminary prospectus is filed with the SEC, the managing underwriter also distributes it to a group of prospective underwriters with an invitation to join a syndicate. The members of the syndicate will share in the risks and rewards of underwriting the issue, although to a lesser extent than the managing underwriter.

6. *Touring* Toward the end of the approval process, the managing underwriter takes the management of the issuing company to selected locations, usually major cities where the investment banking firm has offices, to meet stockbrokers and institutional investors. This is done in an effort to develop interest in the stock.

7. *Setting the Price* The afternoon before the anticipated "effective" date, the company and the firm managing the underwriting decide on the price at which the shares will be offered to the public and bought by the syndicate. The difference between these prices is known as the *gross spread.* It is the underwriting discount and becomes the underwriters' profit. That night the "pricing amendment," which gives the price information, is printed. It is filed with the SEC the next morning.

8. *Becoming Effective*   When the SEC is satisfied that the company has met its requirements, it declares the registration statement "effective." The final prospectus is printed in quantity and distributed by the printer to the list of underwriters in the syndicate. The underwriters later deliver it to their customers, as they are required to do in order to sell the stock legally.

9. *Closing the Deal*   Five business days after the effective date, the company delivers the securities and the underwriter delivers a check. The deal is closed.

Subsequent Public Stock Offerings

Thriving companies may go to the public for money many times after their initial public offering. Usually there is a current, specific need for capital to expand or a strategic plan that will require capital in the future. If money is to be raised for future needs, the timing of a new stock issue may be determined by high current stock prices.

When a company decides to issue more stock to the public, it goes through a process similar to that of an IPO. For a company that is relatively new to the public or that does not raise money often, the process for the second and third stock offerings will be almost identical to that of the first. The one big difference is the pricing of the stock. Because the company's stock has already traded in the market, it has a current price. However, the issue of a new block of stock may initially reduce the value of the stock that is on the market. For this reason, the opening price of the new stock is often set slightly below the price at which the stock is currently trading.

Since 1983 a company with at least $150 million in stock held by outside investors has been able to take advantage of the SEC's Rule 415. This means it can offer stock directly to the public by means of what is called a *shelf registration*. Instead of following all of the steps of an

Account executives at a brokerage firm in West Chester, Pennsylvania. After an investment banking firm brings a stock or bond issue to the public, stockbrokers buy and sell these securities for investors.

UNDERWRITING
SECURITIES

25

IPO and writing a new prospectus, the company simply files a registration statement with the SEC stating how many shares it plans to sell to the public over the next two years and listing the investment banking firms that might underwrite the offerings. The shares that the company intends to issue are said to be "on the shelf." Potential investors are given the registration statement and referred to the prospectus, as well as recent annual or quarterly reports, for financial information about the company. When the company determines that stock market conditions are advantageous, it files a pricing amendment with the SEC. Then it "takes the stock off the shelf" and starts selling it to the public. The reserved shares may be sold all at once or over a period of time, in quantities that the company believes the market can absorb. Shelf registrations have reduced the amount of advisory work by investment bankers for subsequent stock offerings, and consequently the bankers spend less time and earn less from this aspect of their work than from IPOs.

Issuing Bonds

After their initial public offering, many companies raise money from the public by issuing bonds rather than by selling shares of stock. In part this is because it costs more to issue stocks than to issue bonds.

A bond represents a company's debt. The issuing company is borrowing money from the bond buyers. For the privilege of using their money, the company pays interest to the bondholders until the bond's maturity, or due date, at which time the full value of the bond or loan must be repaid.

Corporations are not the only institutions that raise money from the public by issuing securities. States, cities, counties, and their agencies need large amounts of money for construction projects. They often obtain this money by

selling bonds to the public. Whereas corporations issue both stocks and bonds, public agencies raise money only through debt offerings. Their bonds are called municipals, or "munis." Because the interest received by the bond-holders is free from federal, and sometimes state and local taxes, the bonds are also called "tax exempts."

The steps in issuing bonds are similar to those in issuing stocks. Investment bankers underwrite the bond issue and advise the issuer, for which they receive a fee. They sell the bond to the public, for which they collect commissions. And they may trade the security for their own account, making money on price changes and interest when they hold the bond for a significant period of time.

The major difference between stock and bond offerings is that stocks represent ownership shares and bonds represent loans. This leads to differences in pricing, length of time the security may be held, and money received by the

A sample of a bond and its coupons issued by General Motors. One way in which investors collect the interest from their bonds is by clipping the coupons and sending them to the bank that distributes the interest for the company.

UNDERWRITING
SECURITIES

A municipal bond issued by the state of Missouri. States raise money through taxes and bond issues.

security holder. Stocks are issued as units with widely varying prices. In contrast, bonds are usually issued in minimum denominations of $1,000, but may be issued in $5,000 or $100,000 denominations as well. Stocks are held until the shareholder sells them, but bonds are issued with specific maturity dates—perhaps 10, 20, or 30 years into the future. At that time the municipality or corporation pays the face amount of the bond, known as the principal, and the bondholder has no further interest in the government agency or company. Before maturity, bondholders receive interest but not dividends. Bond interest is usually a fixed or specified percentage of the face value of the bond, typically paid twice a year. Stocks, in contrast, pay dividends based on profits.

Two other important ways in which bond issues differ from those of stocks are the role of investment bankers and the lack of a regulating authority. When corporations issue bonds, they choose an investment banker to assist them in preparing a registration statement similar to a stock issue registration statement. However, most municipal bond underwritings begin when the issuing agency prepares a Request for Proposal (RFP), which is sent to investment banking firms all over the country. The firms' representatives respond by submitting information to the issuer. They will describe their success with similar offerings in the past and promote the particular bankers who would work on the deal, hoping to get the issuer to choose them to underwrite the bond issue.

Instead of receiving the approval of the SEC, both corporate and tax-exempt bonds are rated by private companies, either Standard & Poor's or Moody's Investors Service, or both. Bond analysts consider the bond's *credit risk*. This is an evaluation of the bond issuer's reliability, the likelihood that the issuer will pay both interest and principal on schedule. Ratings range from a high of AAA

("Triple A") to a low of C. The lower the rating, the higher the risk. Generally bonds with a low rating will carry higher interest rates in order to attract buyers.

Municipals, which are issued in the same manner as corporate bonds, are designated as either general obligation bonds or revenue bonds. The issuer of general obligation bonds pays interest and principal out of its general funds, which are derived from various sources, especially taxes. Payments due on revenue bonds come from the income derived from the financed project, such as tolls for a highway authority issue.

Bond issues are regulated only by state securities, or "blue-sky," laws. These laws are generally less strict than the state laws regulating common stock and much less strict than SEC regulations for stock issues.

The major effort in issuing bonds consists of negotiations among the interested parties: the issuer, borrower, investment banker(s), and their respective lawyers. During negotiations all of the parties try to agree on an interest rate, maturity date, and other terms that will raise enough money to meet the needs of the borrower and be attractive to investors. Once the terms have been agreed to, the bonds are sold to the public. This may be done either by a syndicate or, increasingly, by the managing underwriter who alone takes on the risk of selling the bonds.

CREATING NEW INVESTMENTS

Since commissions for selling stock were deregulated in 1975, underwriting firms have been competing by rapidly introducing what they call "new products." These are new types of investments designed to please both investors and issuers, as well as to generate fees for the underwriters. There are now hundreds of products that are not strictly stocks or bonds. Several firms have created identical products that go by different names.

Among the earliest products were *zero coupon bonds*, or "zeros." Zeros are bonds that are sold at a sharp discount from their face value, or par value, and pay the accumulated interest when the bond matures (or if it is sold before the maturity date). At that time the owner receives the full face value of the bond as well as all the accumulated interest. A buyer of zeros might pay $700 for a bond and receive $1,000, the face value, 10 years later. U.S. Savings Bonds are a familiar form of zeros.

In the 1980s American corporations began issuing similar bonds, in much larger denominations. From the corporate zeros came the idea of *STRIPS*, an acronym standing for Separate Trading of Registered Interest and Principal of Securities. STRIPS are treasury securities (not savings bonds, but bonds issued by the U.S. Treasury that are traded in the open market) in which the principal or face-value part is separated from the interest part. These two parts may be sold to two different investors. Someone who needs regular income will buy the coupon, receiving regular payments every six months until the bond matures. Someone who prefers to wait a number of years before receiving money from the investment will buy the principal part. Each portion has a present value based on cal-

The bond trading department at the New York office of Merrill Lynch. Merrill Lynch is one investment banking firm that offers new bond products to the investor.

culations of future interest payments. The combined present value of both parts of a STRIP is higher than the original cost of the unstripped treasury bond. The difference in price between the original cost of the entire bond and the combined value of its two portions becomes part of the investment bankers' profit. Investment banking firms have been quite creative in marketing their own versions of STRIPS, giving them such names as TIGRS (Treasury Investment Growth Receipts) and LYONS (Liquid Yield Option Notes), both from Merrill Lynch Capital Markets, and CATS (Certificate of Accrual on Treasury Securities), from Salomon Brothers.

Another new product is a *CMO*, an acronym for Collateralized Mortgage Obligation. CMOs are one type of what are called *mortgage-backed securities. Collateral* is valuable property that is used to guarantee a loan; if the loan is not repaid, the lender has a claim on the property. A CMO is a bond, usually issued by a subsidiary of an investment banking firm, that is backed or secured by a pool or collection of *mortgages.* (Mortgages are loans made by banks or other lending institutions to property buyers.) The mortgages in this pool have as collateral one- to four-family homes and are typically guaranteed by the Government National Mortgage Association (GNMA, called "Ginnie Mae"). An investment banking firm buys the mortgages from the savings banks or savings and loan associations that wrote them. So there is a chain of guarantees supporting a CMO: If the home buyer cannot pay the mortgage, the GNMA or other guarantor will pay. If the issuer cannot pay interest and principal on the bonds, the pooled mortgages, called "Ginnie Maes," in this case, will be used for payment. CMOs are sold in denominations starting as low as $1,000 to attract individual as well as institutional investors. CMOs are a secure investment for investors, and they pay a higher interest rate than comparably secure bonds.

There are now CMO-type investments in which the collateral consists of pools of automobile loans instead of Ginnie Mae-guaranteed mortgages. They are known as CARS (Certificate of Automobile Receivables, created by Salomon Brothers) or FASTBACS (First Automotive Short-term Bonds and Certificates, created by Drexel Burnham Lambert).

Top executives of B. F. Goodrich Co. and Uniroyal, Inc., announce the agreement to merge their tire businesses into a joint venture in January 1986.

MERGERS AND ACQUISITIONS

In the 1980s many prominent businesses changed in shape and size. They did this by acquiring other companies and by divesting (selling off) parts of the original or the combined companies. In 1986 alone, mergers, acquisitions, buyouts, and divestitures made up a $267 billion industry.

Often similar businesses merge, or one acquires the other. In the mid-1980s, for instance, Chevron Oil acquired Gulf Oil. Frequently, though, a company will absorb a different, but possibly related, type of business. This is done in order to diversify, to be able to offer a variety of products in the marketplace. For example, also in the mid-1980s, Philip Morris, a tobacco products company that had earlier acquired 7-Up, bought Standard Brands, which produces grocery products. Acquiring companies have a variety of goals: They may want a company's brand names; access to its new markets; or use of its reserved hoards of cash. There has been debate over the benefit of corporate mergers and acquisitions to the U.S. economy. But there is no question that the boom in this activity has been a gold mine for the investment banking industry. Investment bankers are involved as advisers, helping companies plan strategies and negotiate deals. In the case of what is called an unfriendly takeover, they also help the acquiring company in its attack or the target company in its defense. As

At their annual meeting, share-holders discuss the potential acquisition of their company by another one.

merger and acquisition activity continues, investment bankers are taking a more active role and even commit their firms' own money to help complete a deal.

Different Types of Acquisitions

There are three basic ways in which one company can acquire another: asset deals, mergers, and tender offers.

Asset Deals   In an *asset deal*, the acquirer buys all the assets, including property and other valuables such as patents, but not the stock owned by the target company's shareholders. The acquirer usually agrees to pay the target's liabilities (whatever the company owes). This is a friendly agreement, which means that the management teams of both companies will negotiate with each other to determine the structure of the combined company and the pricing arrangements. In these negotiations different teams of investment bankers and lawyers give advice to each company. After negotiations are completed, an independent investment banker, who has not helped negotiate the agreement, is brought in to give a "fairness opinion" of the arrangements, stating that the deal is financially fair to the stockholders.

(continued on p.35)

MERGERS: TWO CASE HISTORIES

GE/RCA: A Friendly Merger In early 1986 General Electric Company (GE) acquired RCA Corporation (RCA) for $6.3 billion. It was the largest non-oil-company merger in history and resulted in the seventh largest industrial company in the country. GE and RCA both manufactured a variety of products and had in common their contracts for the defense industry.

When its board of directors decided to acquire RCA, GE called an investment banker who set up a meeting with the chief executive of RCA. The timing was right: RCA saw advantages in the merger and agreed to it. RCA's stockholders voted approval.

Six months after the merger announcement, both companies, aided by their investment bankers, had completed the whole transaction. It had been an uncontested deal; there were no defensive moves on RCA's part. The fees of both sets of investment bankers' came to $9 million.

Bendix/Martin Marietta/Allied: A Hostile Takeover Attempt In August of 1982 Bendix, a large corporation with electronics, automobile parts, appliance, and aerospace divisions, made a tender offer to buy the shares of Martin Marietta, another large company with defense and aerospace contracts.

Determined to remain independent, Martin Marietta hoped to discourage Bendix by declaring a counteroffer to buy shares of Bendix's stock. However, Bendix did not back down. While Martin Marietta shareholders were being asked by Bendix to tender, or surrender, their shares, Bendix shareholders were simultaneously being asked to tender their shares to Martin Marietta.

In the end a third company, Allied, bought Bendix. Martin Marietta then arranged with Allied to exchange the Bendix shares it had already acquired for the Martin Marietta stock that Bendix had acquired.

This solution was devised by an investment banker at Kidder Peabody. It brought the stalemate to an end and allowed Martin Marietta to remain independent. However, Martin Marietta was financially weakened because it had borrowed almost $1 billion to purchase Bendix's shares, and soon after it sold off some of its divisions to raise cash. Bendix, the original raider, ceased to function as an independent company. Only Allied survived and prospered. The final takeover involved four investment banking firms, eight law firms, and courts in four states.

(continued from p. 33)

The agreement must be approved by the boards of directors of both companies and then by the shareholders of the acquired company. Shareholders are sent a *proxy statement* explaining the terms of the proposed deal. They are asked to vote their shares for the agreement, either in person, at a meeting to be held approximately four weeks later, or by returning the proxy card with their decision on it. (A *proxy* is a written authorization to someone to represent and vote his or her shares at a shareholders' meeting.) Meanwhile, the investment bankers for both companies contact big stockholders and encourage them to approve the deal.

If the acquisition is approved, a closing is held at which the seller turns over all of its assets to the buyer, and the buyer pays the purchase price to the seller. Then the acquired company liquidates itself by sending a notice to shareholders to return their stock certificates. When they do, they receive their proportional share of the proceeds of the sale.

Mergers A *merger* is a transaction in which two companies combine into a single company, with the acquired company merging fully into the acquiring company and ceasing to exist as an independent entity. As in the asset deal, the companies negotiate, receive a fairness opinion, and gain the approval of both companies' boards of directors and the target company's shareholders. Sometimes the approval of the acquiring company's shareholders is solicited as well.

However, in contrast to an assets deal, no liquidation of the acquired company is required. The company is simply merged into the surviving company when a Certificate of Merger is filed with the appropriate state office. The shareholders of the acquired company are entitled to a proportional share, in stock or money, of the purchase price of the company, which they receive when they return their stock certificates. Then the deal is complete.

Robert R. Frederick, president and CEO of RCA; John F. Welch, Jr., chairman and CEO of GE, and Thornton F. Bradshaw, chairman of RCA, shake hands at the announcement of their merger in December 1985. GE paid $6.28 billion in cash to merge with RCA.

A Tender Offer   Although asset deals and mergers are the most common way in which one company can buy another, there is a third possibility. This is through what is called a *tender offer*. Tender offers are employed when the acquiring company believes that the target company does not want to be acquired. A tender offer is often described as a "hostile takeover."

The acquiring company will try to buy as much of the outstanding stock of the target as possible in order to control votes, and eventually the whole company. To buy up stock, the "raider" usually bypasses the target company's managers and directors and goes directly to the shareholders. The "raider" makes a request to the shareholders to "tender" (formally surrender) their shares in exchange for usually more money than the current market value. The acquiring company must follow certain regulations of the SEC when making a tender offer to shareholders.

The officers, investment banker, and lawyer of the acquiring company prepare the tender offer document, which is filed with the SEC. This is similar to a registration or proxy statement. The "raider" must announce in the tender offer document that the offer is just the first step in a plan to acquire the company and that, if it receives a large proportion of tenders, it will immediately propose a merger on the same terms as the tender offer. The "raider" then places notices in major newspapers stating that it is offering to buy any and all of the shares of the target at $X per share. When the notices are published, the target company is obligated by federal law to mail a copy of the tender offer to all its shareholders. This is to ensure that every shareholder is fully informed about the offer.

The target company may take several steps to defend itself, depending on the advice of investment bankers and lawyers. The target company may send a letter advising shareholders that tendering their shares is not in their best interest. Usually, though, shareholders are tempted by the high price being offered for their shares. The target company may also seek a different and more compatible acquiring company, often called a "white knight." Meetings between these two companies, with their respective investment bankers, might result in a new tender offer, which the target company encourages its shareholders to accept.

Or the target company may make a "counter tender" offer to buy 50 percent of all tendered stock at a higher price than the original offer by the raider. If this works, the defender will survive intact and independent, but with less money (reduced assets) because of the expense of buying its own shares. Other strategies may also be used.

OTHER INVESTMENT BANKING ACTIVITIES

In addition to underwriting and selling different kinds of securities to the public and arranging mergers and acquisitions, investment bankers pursue a long and growing list of other activities. Among the most significant are their involvements with private placements, venture capital, real estate transactions, thrift conversions, and leveraged buyouts.

Private Placements   Any sale of a security that is not an offering to the general public is a *private placement*. Private placements are less expensive and more quickly arranged than are public offerings. Institutional investors such as pension funds, insurance companies, and bank trust departments are major buyers of private placement securities.

The SEC does not require registration of private placements, but does prohibit a private placement from being

OTHER
ACTIVITIES

37

An investment banker visits the construction site of a real estate project financed by his firm.

sold to the general public. Investors in private placements generally cannot sell the securities publicly for two years, and in the third year they may sell them only with restrictions. Thus, the investment is not liquid, or able to be traded freely, for three years. Investors are willing to accept these limitations because private placement securities cost less than those sold to the general public.

Investment bankers serve the issuing company by helping to structure the private placement and by locating suitable investors. They do not, however, underwrite private placements but instead sell them on a "best efforts" basis. That is, the investment banker does not purchase the securities issue but acts as a sales agent for the offering. Any unsold securities are retained by the issuer.

Venture Capital *Venture capital* is money invested to help a new business (venture) in its early stages. This money is used for expansion so that the business can eventually go public. When that happens, the venture capitalists who provided the money can earn hefty profits by selling their stock to the public. Not every venture capital investment is successful, however. One estimate is that 40 percent of these investments lose money. Because venture capitalists take big risks, these entrepreneurs expect to realize large profits on the investments that do pay off.

Investment bankers help bring potential investors and newly formed companies together. They also form venture capital funds to seek out promising new activities. By spreading their investments among several new businesses, venture capitalists minimize the risk of heavy loss from any one investment.

Real Estate Investment bankers' involvement in real estate includes serving as brokers (or agents) for property sellers or buyers and investing the firm's own money in what they hope will be a profitable continuing venture. They may also assemble the money of domestic and foreign investors for use in various projects, either on an individual deal basis, as needed by builders and developers, or by forming a fund that the investment bankers will manage. Investors in these funds are usually corporations and wealthy individuals. However, investment bankers also make large real estate investments available to small investors by selling fund shares in smaller denominations such as $1,000.

Thrift Conversions   *Thrift conversions* involve providing money for savings banks and savings and loan associations, called "thrifts," when the need for capital arises. In such a situation, a thrift institution might convert from being a bank owned privately by its depositors to being a publicly owned stock company. In a thrift conversion, investment bankers play the same advising and underwriting role as in an IPO. However, the process differs slightly because the bank's depositors must vote their approval before the conversion plan can go into effect. The initial offering of stock, called a "subscription," is often made only to depositors and other members of the bank's community.

Leveraged Buyouts   In a *leveraged buyout* (LBO) a company's managers buy the company from its public shareholders and create a privately held company owned by management and those investors who have contributed toward the purchase price. In this situation "leverage" means the ability of managers to control more resources than they actually own. LBOs usually require the new owners to borrow heavily to finance their purchase of the company. The resulting debt is almost always repaid out of the future operating profits of the company.

LBOs can serve as a defense against takeovers: After a company has become private it is no longer subject to hostile tender offers. Investment bankers often suggest an LBO to a company that seems vulnerable to a takeover bid.

The main role of investment bankers in an LBO is to interest additional investors and to arrange the loans and sale of assets needed to raise the money to purchase the stock and take the company private. Recently investment banking firms have been putting up their own money to help finance LBOs.

LAW AND ETHICS IN INVESTMENT BANKING

As a result of abuses and subsequent investigations of the investment industry in the early 1930s, many controls were written into law. These laws and later regulations, which are primarily enforced by the SEC, were intended to ensure fairness for professionals and the involved public. In an industry dominated by institutional investors, it might seem unrealistic for small traders to have the same advantages as big ones. However, that is the goal. In 1986 and 1987 several cases of illegal practices surfaced as a number of investment bankers and others were charged with insider trading and stock price manipulation.

Illegal Activities

Insider Trading An "insider" is someone who is in a position to have information that is not available to the general public. Ethical standards require the information to be kept confidential. Using inside information to make a personal profit (such as buying securities at a lower price and selling them after a merger announcement raises their price) is illegal. Insider trading is forbidden to give equal opportunity to investors who do not have access to privileged information. Because investment bankers know well in advance about proposed mergers, there is supposed to be an impenetrable "Chinese wall" separating the mergers and acquisitions department of an investment firm from its trading department.

The well-publicized scandals of 1986 and 1987 involved activities that were clearly illegal. Merger and acquisition bankers at various firms sold information about forthcoming merger deals to arbitrageurs, stock traders who specialized in *risk arbitrage*. Risk arbitrage is buying the stock of a company that may be about to become a takeover target in order to make a profit when its price goes up. These traders, or "arbs," then bought large blocks of stock, which they soon traded at substantial gain.

Insider trading hurts potential investors because the price of the target's stock has already been pushed up by the arbs' trading activity before the public even learns about the proposed merger. The acquiring company or raider is also hurt because insider trading can force up the target's price. The target company can be hurt in two ways. If it plans to fight the takeover with a "counter tender" for its own stock, a higher price for that stock makes this defense more expensive. Also, arbitragers who control large blocks of stock are more likely to vote or tender their shares based solely on the best price for the stock instead of the best future for the company. And the market as a whole is hurt because investors lose confidence if they believe others have an unfair advantage.

Stock Price Manipulation   Stock price manipulation concerns changes in a company's stock price at the time of a public offering. The underwriters of the stock increase their own buying or induce others to buy it on the day before the offering, thus raising the price of the stock. In one price manipulation in the late 1980s, a firm was asked by an underwriter to buy shares and then "park" or hold them until the offering had been completed at the artificially high price caused by the purchase. The underwriter then sold high, and other investors watched their stock purchase lose value as the price dropped with the large sale.

Although stock manipulation is illegal, many Wall Streeters admit that it is not unusual. As some observers explain, buying to keep the stock price from falling, rather than to raise it, is perfectly legal if the possibility of such a purchase is disclosed in the final prospectus and the transaction is effected in accordance with SEC rules.

In stock manipulation investors are hurt because they must pay a higher price for the stock. The issuing company is hurt when the manipulated price falls soon after the offering, which makes investors dissatisfied with the company and hampers its ability to attract new investors.

Unethical Activities

Insider trading and stock manipulation are both unethical and illegal. More subtle forms of unethical behavior that are technically not illegal involve conflicts of interest or overaggressiveness.

One such conflict can be between an investment banking firm's underwriting client and its stock trading customers, which are usually large institutional investors. The underwriter's contractual relationship is with the issuing company, and it is this company's interest that must remain paramount. Nevertheless, some firms may be tempted to help lower a stock's price slightly to get their big customers a better deal.

Investment bankers also act unethically if they encourage deals that bring in fees but are not in the best interests of the stockholders of the acquiring company. A related conflict of interest may arise when a firm submits a favorable "fairness opinion" for a deal that does not do well by the stockholders. Investment bankers may act unethically if they keep presenting deal ideas to the company's managers, distracting them from doing their best for the business.

Another unethical practice may occur when an investment company decides that a particular company would be an attractive acquisition and tries to solicit potential raiders in the hope of getting business. The firm's trading department may learn that the potential target is "in play" (ready for a takeover), promote sales of its securities, and profit from an increase in stock price. The target may be completely uninterested in a merger deal and could be hurt by the unfounded fluctuations in its stock prices.

In earlier years, when Wall Street had a less competitive environment and fewer people entered investment occupations at a given time, newcomers would learn professional ethics over a period of time, as they worked closely with experienced investment bankers. Today firms are growing so explosively that this type of training can no longer take place.

As a result of recent changes in the investment industry itself, and as a consequence of the increase in illegal activities, Wall Street is in the future likely to be more tightly regulated by government as well as by the industry's own regulatory bodies. There are likely to be stricter and more rigorously enforced rules for ethical behavior as well.

GLOSSARY

acquisition Any process in which one company gains control over another.

asset deal A mutually agreeable transaction in which an acquiring company buys all the assets of another company and usually assumes its liabilities.

"blue-sky" laws State laws that protect investors by prohibiting the misrepresentation of securities. These laws require that specific information be given to prospective investors.

bond A certificate that represents a loan to a company (corporate bond) or government agency (municipal bond). The issuing company (the borrower) pays interest for the use of the money and must repay the entire amount of the bond at a specified time.

boutique A small, specialized brokerage or investment banking firm that researches securities.

CMO Acronym for Collateralized Mortgage Obligation; a bond backed by a collection of mortgages that are guaranteed by the Government National Mortgage Association or another mortgage association backed by the federal government.

collateral Property used to secure a loan and to which the lender has a claim if the loan cannot be repaid.

counter tender A company's offer to its shareholders to buy back a majority of its outstanding stock at a higher price than that of a tender offer being made by another party; intended to offset a tender offer.

deregulation In the securities industry, the 1975 Securities and Exchange Commission ruling that stockbrokers' commissions were to be negotiated by the parties involved instead of being set by the New York Stock Exchange, as previously done.

due diligence The investigation (especially by underwriters) of a company proposing to make a public offering, to verify the accuracy of its prospectus.

face value The dollar value that appears on a bond; the amount the issuing company will pay on the maturity date. *See* par value.

initial public offering (IPO) The first-time sale of a company's stock to the general public. An investment banking firm underwrites the offering.

insider trading Illegal stock transactions that take advantage of confidential information to make a personal profit.

investment banker; investment banking firm A person at an investment banking firm who arranges company financing through securities underwritings and makes other financial arrangements; an organization that helps companies raise money by underwriting new issues of stocks and bonds.

issue The offer of a company's securities for sale; also, the actual shares being sold.

leveraged buyout Conversion of a publicly owned corporation to private ownership through the purchase of outstanding shares of the company's stock by its managers.

merger Any process by which two or more separate companies combine into a single company.

mortgage A loan by a savings bank or other lending institution to the buyer of a home or other property. The designated property serves as security for the loan.

mortgage-backed securities Securities that are backed by a collection of home mortgages. *See* CMO.

par value The stated amount of a stock or the face value of a bond.

private placement Sale of securities to a small number of sophisticated investors instead of to the general public.

prospectus The official public report of a company that must be given to potential buyers of a newly issued stock.

proxy statement Information about votes to be taken at a shareholders' meeting, sent with the notice of the meeting. Votes would be necessary to approve a merger or acquisition of the company. The accompanying proxy card, when filled out, signed, and mailed, constitutes formal authorization for someone to vote on behalf of the shareholder at the meeting.

registration statement The document produced by a company before a public offering of its securities that must be filed with the Securities and Exchange Commission for clearance; includes a prospectus, financial statements, information about the company's operations, and the proposed underwriting agreement.

risk arbitrage The buying of the stock of a company that may soon be taken over in order to make a profit on the expected price increase.

Securities and Exchange Commission (SEC) A U.S. government agency established by Congress in 1934 to regulate the trading of stocks and bonds to protect investors.

share of stock Any of the equal parts into which the entire value, or equity, of a company is divided. It represents part ownership in the company.

shelf registration Registration process for offering stock to the public; available to companies with at least $150 million in stock held by outside investors; bypasses the registration process required for an initial public offering.

stock exchange Market in which securities are sold at prices determined by supply and demand. The New York Stock Exchange, American Stock Exchange, and the over-the-counter market are the major U.S. exchanges.

STRIPS Acronym for Separate Trading of Registered Interest and Principal of Securities; bonds in which the principal part is separated from the interest part, and each part may be sold separately.

syndicate Group consisting of two or more investment banking firms that share the risk of underwriting and reselling shares of a particular issue of stock.

takeover The acquisition of one company by another.

tender offer Process by which an acquiring company attempts to gain control over an unwilling target company by buying as much of the outstanding stock of the target company as is possible. Also called a "hostile takeover."

thrift conversion Change in ownership of a privately held savings bank or savings and loan association to a publicly owned corporation.

underwriting The process of buying newly issued securities from a corporation and reselling them to the public. Investment banking firms underwrite new issues.

venture capitalist An individual who provides money to start or expand a business and is willing to make a risky investment in the hope of making a large profit.

zero coupon bond Bond sold at a discount from its face value that pays no interest until it is redeemed.

FURTHER READING

Bloch, Ernest. *Inside Investment Banking*. Homewood, Ill.: Dow Jones-Irwin, 1986. The economics of all aspects of investment banking.

Hartz, Peter F. *Merger: The Exclusive Inside Story of the Bendix-Martin Marietta Takeover War*. New York: William Morrow, 1985. Detailed and absorbing account that assumes some understanding of mergers and acquisitions.

Hoffman, Paul. *The Dealmakers: Inside the World of Investment Banking*. Garden City, N.Y.: Doubleday, 1984. A collection of episodes in investment banking that focus on firms and personalities.

Securities Industry Association, *Yearbook 1986–87*. New York, 1986. Lists personnel and statistics for all securities companies, including investment banking firms.

"Wall Street's Ethics Crisis." *Institutional Investor*, October 1986, pp. 227–245. Discusses the controversy over acceptable and unacceptable behavior in investment banking and predicts changes that recent episodes will bring to the securities industry.

INDEX

RACHEL S. EPSTEIN, a free-lance writer specializing in business subjects, holds an M.B.A. from New York University. Her articles have appeared in the *Wall Street Journal*, the *Washington Post, Working Woman,* and *Ms.* She is the coauthor also of *Biz Speak: A Dictionary of Business Terms, Slang and Jargon.*

PAUL A. SAMUELSON, senior editorial consultant, is Institute Professor Emeritus at the Massachusetts Institute of Technology. He is author (now coauthor) of the best-selling textbook *Economics.* He served as an adviser to President John F. Kennedy and in 1970 was the first American to win the Nobel Prize in economics.

SHAWN PATRICK BURKE, consulting editor, is a securities analyst with Standard & Poor's Corporation. He has been an internal consultant in industry as well as for a Wall Street investment firm, and he has extensive experience in computer-generated financial modeling and analysis.